May
New York, Manhattan
Town Hall, 43rd st.

FACE IT WITH LOVE
Vasudhaiva Kutumbakam

J. P. Vaswani

Published by:
GITA PUBLISHING HOUSE
Sadhu Vaswani Mission,
10, Sadhu Vaswani Path,
Pune - 411 001, (India).
gph@sadhuvaswani.org

FACE IT WITH LOVE
©2015, J. P. Vaswani
ISBN 978-93-80743-89-9

First Edition

DADA VASWANI'S BOOKS
Visit us online to purchase books on self-improvement, spiritual
advancement, meditation and philosophy.
Plus audio cassettes, CDs, DVDs, monthly journals and books in Hindi.
www.dadavaswanisbooks.org

Printed by:
Thomson Press (I) Limited

FACE IT WITH LOVE
Vasudhaiva Kutumbakam

J. P. Vaswani

Gita Publishing House,
PUNE, (India).
www.dadavaswanisbooks.org

Books and Booklets
by
Dada J.P. Vaswani

CONTENT

CONTENT

66 Only the narrow minded
discriminate by saying:
this one is my own;
the other is a stranger.
For those who live contemplatively
the entire world constitutes
but one family. **99**

- Mahopanishad VI: 72

Let me begin with a story, which is part of the narrative mythology of several cultures in the world!

Once upon a time, an old man lived with his three sons in a village. All his sons were hardworking. But they were egotistical and bitterly divided on all issues. They only argued and quarrelled whenever they came together.

The old man tried his best to unite them but he simply could not succeed. The young men were good, righteous people; but they were the target of the mockery of all the villagers who made fun of their constant fighting and arguments.

Years passed, and the old man fell sick. Even as they all realised that he was on his deathbed, the sons paid no heed to his desperate appeal to them to stay united. But the old man did not give up. He decided to teach them a lesson they would not easily forget.

One morning, the old man called his sons to his bedside. He said to them, "You know that among all our fields and gardens, the mango orchard is my favourite. I would like to leave it to the one who will pass a test that I am going to set for the three of you. Listen carefully to my instructions, for the test is in two parts. First of all, I am going to give each of you a bundle of sticks. You will have to separate each stick and break it into two pieces. The one who breaks the sticks quickly will report to me."

The three sons agreed. They collected the bundles from their father and set to work very quickly. Each bundle had ten sticks. They took each stick apart and in no time all the sticks were broken in two.

"I did it first," claimed the eldest.

"You are a liar," said the youngest. "You pushed me aside to run into father's room, or I would have been there before you."

"Big deal," said the other two. "We broke it even before you did." And a bitter quarrel ensued as to who had done the task first.

The old man said, "Dear sons, only the first part of the game is over. Here comes the second and the tougher part. I will now give another bundle of sticks to all of you. You will have to break the sticks as a bundle, not as separate sticks."

The sons agreed and set about trying to break the bundle. But try as they might, they could not break the bundle. Shamefaced and subdued, they trooped in to tell their father that it could not be done.

The old man said to them, "You see how easy it was to break the sticks when you took them one by one. But when they were tied into one bundle, you could not break them! There is a lesson for you. If you are united, nobody can break you or harm you in any way. If you are divided and keep quarrelling with each other constantly, people can easily defeat you and take advantage of you. My dying appeal to you, therefore, is to stay united!"

The brothers were truly abashed. They realised what it was to be united and promised their father that they would all stay together as a family. In unity is strength!

Therefore the ancients said to us, "Where there is unity, there is always victory." And Franklin D. Roosevelt, a much loved former President of the USA, remarked, "The point in history at which we stand is full of promise and danger. The world will either move forward toward unity and widely shared prosperity – or it will move apart."

The choice is ours: shall we move forward in unity, or move apart in strife and disharmony?

THE
WORLD
IS ONE
FAMILY!

It is a wonderful universe in which we live. A universe in which no man can live alone. It has been rightly said that no man is an island. To live is to be interconnected. Man is a social being and his survival depends on a thousand invisible threads.

This truth is ingrained in the heart of every believing Hindu. The brotherhood of man, the concept of 'All Creation is One Family' is a *given* in the Hindu way of Life.

Werner Heisenberg called the universe a participating universe, one which has meaning and significance only when we relate to it and interact with it.

Interconnectedness is inbuilt in our lives. We take in oxygen from the atmosphere; we use water from the rivers, springs and wells; we derive food from plants and trees.

We inhabit the earth, which is a garden of God. The state of this earth has a direct bearing on our lives; its floods, droughts and unseasonal weather affect our activities.

If the earth is a garden, we are the gardeners, the caretakers. And it is God's garden, everyone's garden! I cannot litter or abuse the garden; for I share it with my people.

This feeling of "my people" applies not only to your blood

relations, but to everyone you meet. A few years ago, an ailing child from Pakistan, Baby Noor, was invited to come to Bangalore in India for a critical heart-surgery. The doctors and nurses at Narayana Hridayalaya where she was operated, fell in love with Noor; indeed, the people of India opened their hearts to Baby Noor and lavished her with their love, their prayers and their gifts. Territorial disputes, tension between diplomats and past wars were all forgotten in the act of people reaching out to their fellow human beings in distress.

I am happy to say that over twenty patients from Pakistan have come to our Sadhu Vaswani Mission's Medical Complex, received free treatment/free surgery and returned home as our friends, friends of India and Indians.

It is sad that we only talk about skirmishes on the border and infiltrations, while people who connect with each other are forgotten!

In my mind, there is no doubt whatsoever that at the most profound level of the spirit, all humanity is closely interconnected.

" World peace cannot be achieved
unless we have first established
unity in the hearts of men. **"**

- J.P.V.

STAYING
CONNECTED

On the spiritual plane, we all are already one. It is only on the physical and emotional plane that we have to work very hard for this unity. Our physical and material existence creates barriers and walls that are difficult to break down. We pump in the idea of 'separation' into the minds of our children as soon as they start thinking; we segregate them into class and caste and status consciousness; we tell them *who* they should play with, *who* they should be friends with and *whom* not to talk to and not to play with. It is so easy to build barriers; it should be equally easy to build bridges!

Long ago, six passengers boarded a boat to cross a river. No sooner had the boat set out, than one of the passengers began to drill a hole on the hull beneath his feet so that he could twirl his toe in the waters. The other passengers were shocked and tried to point out to him that he could sink the whole boat; but he responded blithely and very foolishly that he had paid the full fare for his seat and he could do what he liked with it! None of us can be so foolish as to say along with this man, "What difference does it make to you if I do whatever I like to do?"

One humanity is not a mere mental concept. In deeds of daily living we must bear witness to this great ideal, that we are not apart from each other, we are so many parts of the One Whole. But we regard ourselves as separate from the rest. We create an intellectual, psychological illusion which imprisons us, restricting us to show affection to a few, near to us. We need to grow in the spirit of love and compassion. This is the short cut to world peace.

Jacqueline Novogratz is a social activist and CEO of Acumen, which was started in 2001 with a vision "to transform the world of philanthropy by looking at all human beings not as distant strangers, but as members of a single, global community where everyone had the opportunity to build a life of dignity". In her book, The Blue Sweater, *she tells us how her uncle presented her a blue sweater with Mount Kilimanjaro knitted right across the front, and her name embroidered on the back. The gangling teenager was so fond of the sweater that she wore it to school almost everyday, right into her High School, even when it became uncomfortably tight for her. In her final year, a teacher passed a very unkind and insulting remark about the tight sweater. She went home in tears, told her mother all about it and threw the sweater into the garbage bin.*

Time passed. Jacqueline went into Rwanda on an assignment and on an early morning walk one day, she saw a little boy walking towards her (he was just a little 'pipsqueak') wearing the same blue Kilimanjaro sweater that she had thrown away, hoping never to see it again. On closer inspection it was revealed that it was her sweater, with her name embroidered on the back collar. Jacqueline recalls that she understood in a flash what human interconnectedness was all about! She tells us that the unbelievable encounter with the past, the whole experience of seeing the sweater again, was a metaphor for interconnectedness and she understood how our actions and reactions impact hundreds of people whom we might never see all our lives!

"If mankind was created by God,
is not our brotherhood
an established fact?**"**

- J.P.V.

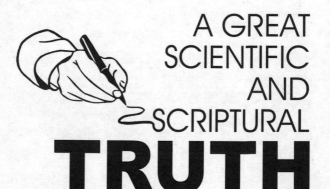

A GREAT
SCIENTIFIC
AND
SCRIPTURAL
TRUTH

All of us, human beings, living in every corner of this earth – Blacks, Whites, Brown and Yellow-skinned people, Europeans, Asians, Chinese and Americans – belong to one species, Homo sapiens.

Scientists now believe that Homo sapiens evolved in Africa 200,000 years ago. Like other early human species living at that time, they gathered and hunted food, and evolved behaviours that helped them to survive. They learnt to make and use stone tools; they also devised bows and arrows, fish hooks and harpoons to respond to the challenges of an unstable environment. In the process, the human brain evolved.

Our ancestors made the transition to growing plants for food and changing their surroundings. The hunter became a farmer and the landscape of Planet Earth began to be transformed. Settlements became villages, towns and then cities.

Modern humans evolved a unique combination of physical and behavioural characteristics, some of which may have been present in humans of ancient species, but not to the same degree. They developed complex brains that enabled them to interact with each other and with their environment in meaningful and novel ways.

We might say that it was their more developed brains that

helped our ancestors survive. They developed new and specialised tools; built shelters for themselves; they built social networks and created art and music... This was "the great leap forward" in human evolution.

We have come a long way since then; but it is sad that we are so obsessed with our differences today that we have forgotten our common human origins!

Why is it that we cannot speak of rights without responsibilities? Why is it that we cannot speak of freedom without peaceful co-existence, respecting the freedom of others? It is because we are members of one large family of humanity. In the words of Martin Luther King, Jr. "We are caught in an inescapable network of mutuality, tied in a single garment of destiny. Whatever affects one directly, affects all indirectly. This is the interrelated structure of all reality. You can never be what you ought to be until I become what I ought to be."

We all are, always have been, and always will be interdependent. We may not have uniformity; but we must have unity; diversity will always be there, but it must be respected and appreciated. When we respect and appreciate differences, it enhances our uniqueness and our distinctions.

In Hindu mythology, Lord Brahma is said to have divided

himself in half to create Manu and Shatarupa, the first Man and Woman who became the parents of humanity.

In Greek mythology, Gaia (the Earth) and Uranus (the Sky) became the progenitors of the first race of Titans.

Common to Abrahamaic religions is the story of Adam and Eve whom God created to inhabit the Paradise called Eden, which He created exclusively for them. He wanted them and their offspring to live happily ever after in Eden, but they were driven out of Paradise due to their sin of disobedience.

Homo sapiens had the same ancestors; they evolved from one species.

This is not a revolutionary new idea that I am expressing! Our ancient *Rishis* spoke thousands of years ago about the concept of *vasudaiva kutumbakam*—the world as one family. The Tamil Sangam poets of the 3rd Century AD sang, "Every place is my home; everyone is my relative!"

No other world scripture expresses the spirit of universal brotherhood as beautifully as the Vedas:

> *Om sarvesham svastir bhavatu*
> *Sarvesham shantir bhavatu*
> *Sarvesham poornam bhavatu*
> *Sarvesham mangalam bhavatu*

Auspiciousness be unto all,
Perfect peace be unto all,
Fullness be unto all,
Prosperity be unto all.

Sarve bhavantu sukhinah,
Sarve santu niramayah
Sarve bhadrani pasyantu
Maa kaschit dhukha bhag bhavet
Om, Shantih, Shantih, Shantih!

May all be prosperous and happy
May all be free from illness
May all see good in everything
May no one suffer!
Om, Peace, Peace, Peace!

What a wonderful, universal prayer this is!

The ancient *Rishi* boldly declared: "The world is my country and to do good is my religion!"

❝ There is but One Life in all!
The One Life sleeps in the mineral and the stone,
stirs in the vegetable and plant,
dreams in the animal and wakes up in man. **❞**

- J.P.V.

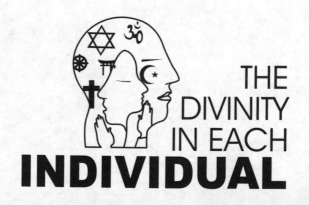

THE
DIVINITY
IN EACH
INDIVIDUAL

It is an underlying tenet of Hindu belief that the entire Cosmos is animated by the Divine; and it is this same Divine spark that illumines the soul, the *atman* of man. And this Divine spark is found in the inner being of every man, woman and child, irrespective of his or her race, religion, culture or country of birth! Every human being is imbued with the divine spark; with divine potential! This is why we have the typical Indian greeting with palms joined in reverential salutation: the beautiful greeting *Namaste* with what we call the *Anjali mudra* which literally means, "I bow to the Divine in you!"

There was an ashram *which had grown and flourished as a spiritual sanctuary to many; but it fell upon bad days when differences began to crop up between members who had till then been united in their ideals and values. The holy* sanyasi *who founded the* ashram *had passed away. He had already appointed his own successor, a quiet and gentle monk. The new head monk was determined to follow his master's teachings in letter and spirit, and keep up all the traditions of the* ashram. *But this did not come to pass. The once united fellowship began to fall apart and many disciples and devotees left the* ashram *in disillusionment.*

There was something missing in the ashram *now; petty politics and quarrels entered the* ashram; *the younger monks and the* brahmachari *disciples could not see eye to eye; arguments and quarrels became the order of the day, the staple of all important meetings. Soon the* ashram *became a deserted place; only fifteen to twenty people remained – the head monk, the chief disciples and the people in charge of the day-to-day running of the ashram.*

The chief monk was deeply saddened. Determined to salvage the precious spiritual inheritance of his beloved Master, he decided that he would seek the counsel and wisdom of a holy sage who lived in Rishikesh. This sage had visited the ashram in its flourishing days, and had struck up an immediate rapport with the sanyasi. The chief monk now felt that he would be the right person to offer a remedy to the problems of the ashram.

Arriving at the sage's kutiya in Rishikesh, he was warmly welcomed by the holy man. Soon after his arrival, he sought a private meeting with the sage, and poured out his heart to the seer, begging him to help the ashram from disintegrating altogether.

The sage listened quietly to the chief monk's story. He heard all the details, all the goings-on among the chief disciples and monks. At the end of the meeting, he advised the monk to retire for the night after spending some time in quiet prayer. "I shall do likewise," he said, "And we shall see, the new day will bring with it, God's guidance to tackle the problem. Come to me soon after the morning prayer, and I shall tell you what I think."

The chief monk followed the sage's advice. He spent an hour or so in silent prayer; he prayed fervently to God and his guru, that it must never become his misfortune to preside over the closure of his beloved guru's ashram.

Next morning, he was ready and waiting outside the sage's kutiya, *and was summoned soon enough. The sage looked him squarely in the eye, and said to him, "You must go back to the* ashram *and take every step that you can think of to revive it to its former glory. For I say to you, it is not the place you take it to be. The Lord has chosen your* ashram *to appear in one of His secret incarnations. Right now, Lord Vishnu is with you in your* ashram. *He is one amongst you, though you may not be able to perceive Him with your clouded vision. But when the veil falls from your eyes, you will surely see Him. Right now, my message to you is this: by no means must you drive away the Lord from your midst, by your petty quarrels and internal politics. Unite to rebuild your* ashram; *make it a worthy abode of the Lord who has chosen to come amongst you. Return to the* ashram *at once, and set an example to your disciples. Remember, God is with you; He is watching you; He is watching over you."*

The chief monk was speechless with amazement. Lord Vishnu was amongst them, in the ashram! *Who could He be? One of the monks? One among the* brahmacharis? *One of the staff? Try as he might, he simply could not 'place' the chosen man. Each and every inmate of the* ashram *seemed to him to be deeply flawed, and quite, quite unfit to be the secret incarnation of the Lord. But then the Lord was the King of a thousand* leelas: *it was a small matter for him to disguise His omnipotence and omniscience, and appear to the world as an ordinary human being with all the common weaknesses of such a man. He could be a monk; He could be a disciple; He could even be the cook or the watchman or the manager!*

When the chief monk returned to the ashram, *he was a changed man. He was no longer the withdrawn, aloof monk who was content to let things drift from bad to worse. He was a man with a mission: to ensure that the Lord who had come to live in his* ashram, *should not leave the place in disgust!*

When they sat down for their evening prayer, the chief monk cast his eyes round furtively, trying to spot the Lord. Everyone's heads were bowed down in prayer; anyone of them could be the Lord, he thought to himself. Each and every member looked saatvic, *devout and sincere. "I will not let my guru's congregation disperse," he vowed to himself. "It must be my Guru who has pleaded with the Lord to come down amongst us so that we may change our ways and become worthy of His grace."*

There was such a pronounced change in the chief monk's demeanour and attitude that it had a very powerful effect on the rest of the inmates. Suddenly, the vibrations changed; the atmosphere grew more peaceful and positive. It was not long before the chief monk shared his 'intelligence' with the senior monks and disciples. Everyone was spellbound. They began to look at each other with respect and love. If the Lord was indeed amongst them, they were determined that they would give Him no cause to reject their devotion. And since it was impossible to fathom His leelas *and decipher His real identity, they felt that the only thing they could do under the circumstances was to treat everyone with the greatest love and respect. Why, He had come upon this earth as a fish, a tortoise, a boar and a man-lion; He could be the cook, the* watchman, *the manager or indeed one of the* brahmacharis! *There was only one thing to do now: pour out all their love, affection and respect for each and every inmate so that the Lord was sure to receive His due!*

Needless to say that the *ashram* became once again, a centre of radiance, devotion, love and *atma shakti*.

Each one of us is a spark of the Divine! The sooner we realise this interconnectedness, the happier our lives would be!

One day, I was out on a walk with a few of my friends. A man brushed past us, walking in a hurry. Our eyes met only for a second, and I folded my hands in greeting. The man was under such stress that he continued on his way without a response.

One of my friends said to me, "Dada, you greeted him with a *namaste* and he did not even return your greeting!"

My reply was, "I fold my hands only to pay obeisance to the God who resides within everyone, and not to greet the outer form!"

TODAY'S
GLOBAL
CITIZEN

If the Divine animates each one of us, are we not all part of one great consciousness, one great world family? Thousands of years ago, when human beings were blissfully free from the concepts of international travel and visas and resident permits, at a time when the longest distance a traveller could hope to cover was no more than a few miles per day, our scriptures spoke of essential human unity. This is a truth that our ancients have always known; it is a truth that is being just discovered in the West after Einstein and Heisenberg. This is not to establish our superiority over the rest; it is just to emphasise our basic values and beliefs.

Gurudev Sadhu Vaswani often said, "Children of the earth, ye all are one."

The wounded soul of humanity has piteously cried for peace, through the ages. There will be peace among the nations, only if we realise that we all are children of the One Mother – Humanity! We all are human beings. We do not belong to niches and corners and regions, we are global citizens enjoying multiple citizenships – consumer citizenship; flexible citizenship; even mobility citizenship; but in Vedic terms, we are, and always have been members of the One Family of God's Creation!

Experts on the subject tell us that it is technology, capital, flow of travel, trade and human potential that define global citizenship. Together, they constitute a new sense of belonging, a new sense of unity and a loyalty to a broad common ideal of humanity at large. But in India, we have a different 'take' on this.

The Rig Veda tells us: "Let noble thoughts come to us from everywhere."

The idea here is that we are essentially spiritual beings – not the bodies we 'wear' as outer garments. This is our real identity – not our race, or religion, or skin colour! The soul (*atman*) transcends all these divisions.

When we respect everyone's spiritual identity, we promote peace and happiness for all. This is why India has welcomed so many races and religions from ancient times. We don't believe in fighting or dying for our religion; but we would aspire to live up to the ideals our religion places before us!

This is how the Atharva Veda proclaims this truth:

We are birds of one nest;
We wear different skins;
We speak different languages, believe in different faiths;
But we share one home – the earth;
We are all born on this planet;

The same sky covers us;
We gaze at the same stars;
We breathe the same air;
   ...
We may live individually
But we can survive only collectively.

MANAV DHARMA
THE
RELIGION
OF
HUMANITY

Our way of life emphasises the truth that all Humanity is One and that we must respect all faiths and cultures. Truth is One, but the Sages call it by many Names. *Samabhava, samadhrishti*, equality and common vision are embedded in our value systems.

Did you know that what we now refer to as Hinduism or *sanatana dharma* was also known as *manava dharma* or the Religion of Humanity? Religious, linguistic, cultural diversity is a reality in the daily lives of all urban centres in the world today. It is only our faith in our shared humanity that will enable us to live in peaceful coexistence under such conditions of diversity. Our ancient scriptures and the great truths they enshrine give us the faith and the insights that will enable us to live happy, harmonious lives under all such changing conditions. There is no room for feelings about an alien, foreigner or 'other' in the global village.

In the Ramayana, there is a beautiful incident of Vibeeshana Saranagati: it happens at a time when Sri Rama and the Vanara Council are actually discussing the strategy to take on the mighty Ravana and defeat him. At this point, Vibeeshana sends his trusted emissaries to tell Sri Rama that he has come to take refuge with him.

The Lord knows his mind; He knows what He must do. Yet He consults his generals, the Vanara King, Sugreeva, and leaders like Jambvhavan, Angada and Hanuman.

Sugreeva and his Ministers look at the issue rationally. It is the eve of their do-or-die war; here is someone from the enemy camp, in fact, the younger brother of their arch foe; how can such a person be given refuge – what we call in modern terms, political asylum? Promptly they warn Sri Rama that Vibeeshana must not be trusted. It is not just that he must be turned away, but captured and kept in confinement. He is a rakshasa; he is Ravana's own brother; how can Sri Rama accept such a man's plea for friendship and asylum?

Hanuman has a different approach. Alone among everyone present, he has seen Vibeeshana and had the opportunity to judge him. "Ravana is a rakshasa and has demonic traits," Hanuman tells Sri Rama. "But so far as I could see, Vibeeshana's nature was inherently dharmic."

Having heard everyone's views, Sri Rama tells them, "It does not matter whether it is friend or foe, stranger or acquaintance; it is my duty to offer refuge to anyone who comes to me for asylum." In certain versions of the Ramayana, the Lord adds: "Even if it had been Ravana who had come to me for refuge, I would have forgiven him and accepted him."

Notions of enemy, stranger, alien and others are unacceptable to the Lord!

Vibeeshana falls at Sri Rama's feet with tears flowing from his eyes. Sri Rama embraces him and proclaims that Vibeeshana will be the King of Lanka. In fact, then and there, at the Ram Setu seashore, the Lord performs the coronation of Vibeeshana as the King of Lanka. In this wonderful gesture, the Lord has made it clear that he has no territorial ambitions on Lanka; that the outcome of the war is well known to him; it is not just enemy or friend, alien or foreigner, but any sincere soul who approaches him with love and devotion, who will attain to salvation! Thus the Lord demonstrates one of my favourite beliefs: we all are equal in His eyes!

What can help us achieve this sense of shared values and common humanity is the undeniable fact that all faiths, all cultures hold the same underlying values of man's relation to God and the interconnectedness of all creation. This interconnectedness is also stressed in the *Isa Upanishad*: that the entire cosmos with all that is and moves, is pervaded by the Divine.

THE
ORIGIN
AND
CONCEPT
OF THE GLOBAL
FAMILY!

Vasudhaiva Kutumbakam has been much used, much quoted in recent times. Educational institutions have made this their motto; trading houses and commercial organisations too, have made it their vision statement. Politicians of various hues, statesmen, diplomats, foreign policy makers and even peace activists have taken recourse to this great belief so beautifully enunciated in the sacred *Mahopanishad.* This is one of the lesser known *Upanishads* although the particular *sloka* that we have quoted above is one of the most well-known from the Hindu scriptures. This now famous phrase is repeated in variant forms in many subsequent texts including the *Hitopadesha, Panchatantra* and others.

Interestingly, the *Mahopanishad* records a dialogue between the young *jignasu,* Nidhaga and his Guru, Sage Ribhu. After due process of learning at the Guru's feet, Nidhaga had gone on a pilgrimage, taking a sacred dip in countless holy places. But he remains in doubt, tossed by anxiety and worry. He tells his Guru, "I now realise, that the *Shastras* are a burden to one who lacks spiritual discrimination; knowledge is a burden to one who is still attached to the material world; the mind is a burden to one without stability; this very existence in physical form is a burden to one who is not aware of the true Self. Therefore, O, Wise preceptor, awaken me to the Truth with your *tattwa jnana upadesh* " (discourse of true philosophy).

In his kindness and wisdom, Sage Ribhu instructs his disciple on the Seven Steps to *moksha* or *nirvana*. The gist of his teaching is this: Enlightenment can only be achieved in a state of detachment. The man who has attained the state of *brahmistiti* (self-realisation) has no likes and dislikes, no favourites and antagonists. To such a one the entire world is one family!

"You will realise the Self and hold the state of Bliss," the Guru assures Nigadha. "You will know that the Self is in all; that you are the Self; this world is the Self and all created and manifested beings are the Self. You will reach the state of certitude and become established in the Self."

Thus, the doctrine of *vasudhaiva kutumbakam* is recommended by the Sage as a discipline to achieve bliss and self-realisation!

For the next citation of this Upanishadic statement, we must go to the *Panchatantra,* one of the oldest and famous collection of fables from India, attributed to Acharya Vishnu Sharma and thought to have been composed in Sanskrit around the 3rd Century BCE. It was subsequently translated into several world languages including Pali, Pehlavi, Persian, as well as Hebrew, Arabic, Greek, Latin, Tibetan and Chinese. Indeed, many compendiums of fables in these languages are directly indebted to the *Panchatantra*.

I am afraid the reference in this text to our *sloka* is not exactly complimentary. It is the story of four brahmin scholars, entitled, "The Lion that Sprang to life".

Four young brahmins live in a village; three have studied the shastras *rigorously and have become experts in the ancient texts; the fourth one is not so learned, but a man of common sense.*

The four friends decide to leave the village and seek their fortune in the city, where their learning would be valued and appreciated. The three clever ones have a moment of doubt regarding their friend who is not learned in the shastras; *of what use would it be to take him along?*

The first brahmin points out that he has no learning to speak of; the second brahmin agrees that he should in fact, remain behind in the village; but the third one quotes the sloka *we have discussed earlier: all the earth is one family. Let us not discriminate; let us take our friend along. And in the end they decide that their friendship should be respected and even if the ignorant brahmin cannot earn a lot of money, the other three would support him with their earnings.*

And so the four friends set out. Their path passes through the depths of a jungle, where they discover the carcass of some long dead creature. Excited, one of them suggests that they should now put their considerable scholarship to the test and make the dead animal come to life.

The fourth friend (the ignorant man) is alarmed at the suggestion. But his protests are ignored as he is not learned. Quickly, the first brahmin who knows human anatomy, assembles the bones together, and forms the dead animal's skeleton. The second covers the skeleton with flesh and skin. The third brahmin (the one who recited our sloka) quickly prepares to utter the mantra that would bring the creature to life.

The fourth man now protests that the assembled creature resembles a lion; if they were to revive it to life, it would surely devour them all! The others ridicule him. "After reaching so far, we will not throw away the fruits of our knowledge!" they admonish him. "You ask us to desist because you are jealous of our scholarship!"

The fourth brahmin realises the futility of arguing with his learned friends. "Just give me a minute," he begs them. "I will climb to the top of the tallest tree I can find, before the lion springs to life."

He climbs a nearby tree and watches in awe as the third brahmin prepares to breathe prana into the carcass to bring the lion to life. It is accomplished in a trice and even as the three learned brahmins are celebrating their phenomenal success, the lion pounces on them and kills them!

The point made by some people is that this tale subverts the entire concept of the whole world being one family, as the idea is put into the mouth of someone who is impractical and foolish!

The World is One Family!

IS THIS A PRACTICAL IDEAL?

I have narrated two different stories, which seem to contradict each other on the intrinsic truth and validity of our *sloka*. Not that this shakes my faith in this great Vedantic truth: for this is indeed central to Hindu belief, that God is One and all His Creation is one Family!

What are the 'subversion' theorists trying to tell us – that the idea of the world as one family, the idea of Universal Brotherhood is impractical or unrealistic? If this is so, how is it that we accept at its face value, the trade and marketing notion of a 'global village' where all of us can buy and sell from each other? For commerce, yes, but for human relationships, no?

Then again, people point out, even families with their own blood relations are no longer united entities these days. Brothers fight brothers in court; property disputes leave parents and children as bitter enemies. The classic example of this is in the *Mahabharata* where kinsmen fight and kill each other. One venerable elder even observed sadly, that if a husband and wife live together under the same roof today, theirs can be called a 'joint' family!

The fundamental values of our society are being eroded with the fragmentation of families and the rejection of old people—and 'unwanted' children. For, one end of the spectrum has seen the proliferation of old age homes and shelters; and at the other end, our orphanages are also overflowing with abandoned children—especially girl children, who, it seems, are really children of a lesser god! Why else would their own mothers abandon them on rubbish heaps and street corners?

Yes; in the history of human civilisation, brother has killed brother; son has killed mother; wife has killed husband and father has killed son. But that has not destroyed the great institution we call the family. Thousands upon thousands of families live serene, peaceful lives within the four walls of their homes.

Now, the time has come for us to think beyond the walls of our homes; the time has come for us to relate to the larger reality of the planet we live in; it is time we thought of others.

Think of a Sunday lunch or dinner around your family table. Good, wholesome food is set on the table. Will any one of your family members ever dream of taking away all the bread or all of the vegetables for themselves without thinking of others? And yet this is what is happening in the world today. We are told that the world produces enough to feed ten billion people; and yet thousands upon thousands of children are starving or malnourished. And thousands upon thousands of others are eating their way to high cholesterol and diabetes!

I often think that if there is enough love in our hearts and lives, we would never ever eat too much, waste food or insist on extravagant variety in our food. For our love would make us realise that it is our brothers and sisters who are starving while we over indulge! As Mahatma Gandhi said, "The world has enough to satisfy everyone's need, but not enough to satisfy everyone's greed."

Statistics proclaim that there are more millionaires in the world, than ever before. We no longer talk about very rich people; we now talk about HNWI—High Net Worth Individuals, whose disposable income and spending power are increasing phenomenally.

Unfortunately, it is not only people's spending power that has grown; poverty is growing too, side by side. And if HNWIS are on the rise, people classified as BPL—Below Poverty Line—are also multiplying.

The result is that the gap between the haves and have-nots has widened, and everywhere in the world, the rich are getting richer and the poor are getting poorer. While economists and bankers are talking about 'growth' and booming economies, people are still dying of malnutrition and avoidable diseases!

THE
GLASS
OF
MILK

A poor boy who was selling goods from door to door to earn his school fees, found himself famished and exhausted. Afraid that he might faint out of hunger, he decided that he would pick up courage and ask for a meal at the next house he called on.

As luck would have it, a very sweet young lady opened the door. But the little boy lost his courage, and could only stammer, "Can I get a glass of water, please?"

The young lady took one look at him and realised that he was very hungry. She brought him a glass of milk instead. The grateful boy drank the milk up in a trice, and asked shyly, "How much do I owe you for this?"

The young lady smiled kindly. "You owe me nothing! My mother has taught us that there is no price on kindness."

Howard Kelley never ever forgot that incident. Years later, when he had become a well known surgeon, the kind young lady was admitted to his hospital with a serious ailment. Kelley recognised her as soon as he saw her, although she did not realise the identity of the senior surgeon who came to see her. He went all out to save her life and personally supervised the complicated surgery and treatment she needed. He told the Accounts Department to send her bill to him for approval.

When the hefty bill arrived, he paid it in full and sent it to the lady with a brief note at the bottom.

The lady opened the bill with trepidation. She knew that she would have to struggle to pay the bill, probably for the rest of her life. Imagine her joy and gratitude when she read the note scrawled at the bottom of the bill in the surgeon's own handwriting: "Paid in full with one glass of milk. Signed, Dr. Howard Kelly."

This is the power of love, compassion and kindness. Who says it must be confined to our own flesh and blood?

"There is a happiness above happiness. It belongs to him who, forgetting himself, gives happiness to others!**"**

- J.P.V.

HEAVEN
AND
HELL

As little children, we are told that heaven and hell are 'places' that we will go to after our death. As adults, we continue to believe, that we will be transported to these 'places' when we die. But saints and sages tell us that heaven and hell are states of consciousness, conditions of the mind. Even while we live on this earth, we can live in a hell or heaven of our own making.

There was a man who often thought about life after death. One night, he dreamt a strange dream in which he had a vision of hell and heaven.

First, he dreamt that he visited hell. He was astonished to find thousands of people there, with a delicious banquet spread out before them. Every tasty dish, every gourmet delicacy that you and I could dream of, was laid out in that astonishing spread he beheld in 'hell'.

But to his amazement, he saw that the occupants of hell were thin, emaciated and starving! Not a morsel of the delicious food could they lift and put into their mouths! They stared longingly at the veritable feast spread out before them; they even lifted a morsel or two – but try as they might, they could not take it into their mouths to feed themselves.

Looking closely, the man saw something peculiar – every one of the occupants of hell had arms which were straight as rods. Their arms could not be bent. And so it was that though they could pick the food up in their hands, they could not bend their arms and take it to their mouths.

The man saw this, and was shocked! Little had he imagined that hell would be such!

Next, he visited the heaven world. A very familiar sight greeted him there, too. All the people had straight arms, which could not be bent; and the same delicious feast was laid out before them.

"But what is the difference between heaven and hell?" asked the man in astonishment.

"Look closely," said an angel who happened to pass by.

It was then that the man saw that the occupants of heaven were happy, smiling, cheerful and blooming with good health. They picked up the morsels of the delicious food and fed it to their friends around them. True, their arms could not be bent, but they could easily reach across to the others around them. True, no one could feed himself – but the people around them took good care to see that each one was fed. NO ONE was feeding himself; everyone was feeding another.

"Nothing for myself, everything for others." If this were the motto of your life, you would surely live in heaven on earth!

It was Albert Einstein who said, *"Only a life lived for others is worth living."* We can also add, *"Only a life of giving and sharing is worth living."*

" What a wonderful place this world
would be if we were to say to one another,
"You first! I last!" **"**

- J.P.V.

THE
GREAT GIFT
OF
SHARING AND
CARING

How can the world be peaceful and prosperous if one fraction of its people live in luxury and opulence while the majority live in poverty and deprivation? Therefore, we must all learn to share what we have with others!

King Rantideva was a great devotee of Lord Vishnu. The Lord it is said, once mentioned to Indra, Vayu, Varuna and other devas, *that Rantideva was his most beloved and dedicated* bhakta. *The* devas *were taken aback and also intrigued by this firm assertion of the Lord. They decided to test this chosen devotee.*

Rantideva was not only a devout soul but also a good ruler. His kingdom was peaceful and prosperous. Trade and agriculture flourished and the people were happy under his benign rule.

Vayu, Varuna and Indra changed all that! Unseasonal rains, floods and storms ravaged the kingdom; this was followed by a year of severe drought and famine. The people were devastated. Rantideva opened up his royal granaries and food stores; he spent all the money in the royal treasury to see that his people did not starve; he opened up his palace to accommodate refugees and people fleeing from deserted villages. And still the famine spread and the people were plunged in misery; the entire kingdom seemed to be under a terrible curse.

With whatever food grains were left in the palace, Rantideva began a public feeding for one and all. At first rice, rotis and then, as the stocks dwindled, gruel began to be served to every man, woman or child who came to the palace in hunger. The king and his family ate whatever they were served, with them. But still the gods did not relent, and the situation in the kingdom continued to worsen.

Rantideva realised that his faith was being tested. He prayed to Lord Vishnu to save his subjects and decided to go on a fast till the kingdom revived. For 48 days he ate no food, took no water, until he was reduced to bare skin and bones.

Alarmed, the royal family and his ministers begged him to break his fast so that they would not lose his guidance and counsel. He agreed reluctantly, and a small bowl of gruel was brought to the emaciated king. When he was about to take a morsel to his mouth, a man tottered towards the King and said, "Royal sire! I am starving! I have had nothing to eat for a week!"

In a trice, the king offered him the bowl of gruel and said to him, "Eat this, dear brother. It will revive you."

The queen offered the king her share of the gruel. Just as he was about to eat, another hungry man entered the palace, begging for food. In turn, the two princes offered their share of gruel to the king and in turn, he gave it away to a poor man. Now, the little princess offered her bowl. At that very moment a man came in with two dogs; having eaten half the gruel, he offered the remaining portion to his dogs and praised the king for his compassion.

Now, there was no food left to offer to the king and the royal family were also left to go hungry. In despair, they brought some water for the king to drink. As he was about to drink it, a distraught man entered the room, crying, "Water, water! For God's sake give me water, for I am parched with thirst!" Instinctively, the king went to him and offered water, saying, "Drink brother, drink this!"

The man shrunk from his touch and said, "Your Majesty! I am a chandala. *How can I take this from your hands?"*

"Dear brother, you and I are one," said the king. "In you I behold an image of Lord Vishnu! Quench your thirst with this water."

And a miracle came to pass. The chandala *disappeared; and Lord Brahma appeared with the* devas *before the astonished gathering. Lord Vishnu came amidst them, and Rantideva fell at the Lord's feet. Lord Vishnu explained that it was the* devas *who had put him to the test and had appeared as the starving men to take his food away; Lord Yama himself, the god of death had come as the* chandala, *to put him to the final test.*

"My dear Rantideva," Lord Vishnu said to him, "the devas *refused to believe me when I told them that you were my most beloved devotee. You have proved your worth to them now."*

The kingdom was restored to normalcy and the people were saved. As for Rantideva, the Lord granted him liberation and union with Him!

THE
GIFT OF
SERVICE

Can we share all that we have with others? To some of us, this may at first appear a very difficult thing to do! But we will find eventually, that in the measure in which we share what little we have with others, we will be truly blessed—and this world will be a better place for our humble endeavours!

In true giving, in what Sri Krishna describes as *satvic dana*, there is no subject and object, no giver and receiver! The moment you think you are the giver, your giving is vitiated. When you cultivate the consciousness that the giver and receiver are one, then you truly give!

There was a man of God, an ascetic, who lived under a tree outside a village. He rarely left his seat, except to go to the river for his bath. The villagers who passed by would leave a little food for him; he ate whatever he got; if he got nothing, he was content to starve.

One day, a wealthy man happened to pass by in his chariot; he was so moved by the sight of the holy man sitting with his eyes closed in deep meditation, that he left some gold coins, a few delicacies and sweets that he was carrying with him and some fruits as an offering to the ascetic. Through all this, the ascetic did not so much as open his eyes; the wealthy man made his offerings and went on his way.

A little later, the ascetic opened his eyes and saw the offerings left for him. However, he was not hungry at that point and continued to meditate. Suddenly a bunch of ruffians who were passing by, saw the gold and the food left before the holy man and decided to take everything away from him. In the commotion they made, the ascetic opened his eyes; the ruffians beat him up and tied him to the tree, took the food and the gold and ran away.

Towards the evening, the wealthy man was returning home, and was shocked to see the holy man badly beaten up and lying unconscious under the tree. A few coins and fruits were scattered around; the wealthy man surmised what had happened. As he could not revive the ascetic, he asked his men to carry him and place him in the chariot. He drove home and sent for his personal physician to come and attend to the ascetic. After some time, the holy man opened his eyes, and the wealthy man brought a bowl of sweetened milk and fed him with his own hands.

Gradually, the holy man revived and in a weak and trembling voice, he thanked his kind benefactor. His host was still upset and demanded of the holy man, "Tell me, who was it that beat you up? How could anyone be so evil and impious as to harm a holy man like you? Do you know those men? Can you identify them?"

The sanyasi looked at his host and smiled. "He who gave me gold and food and fruits, was the one who robbed me and beat me up; he was also the one who brought me home, tended me like a brother and fed me sweet milk."

The rich man was shocked. "But holy sire, I gave you the gold and the food and the fruits; the ruffians were the ones who beat you up, robbed you and ran away; it was again I who brought you home and attended to you. How can you say it was I who beat you up?"

The holy man smiled. "This is the Lord's leela," he said softly. "He sends someone to beat me up and he sends someone to help me. Aren't you all His children?"

The way of service is closely allied to the way of brotherhood—for we need to assert, again and again, "I am my brother's keeper!"

And who are our brothers? Our brothers and sisters are all those who suffer and are in need of help—men, women, birds and animals. We must become channels of God's mercy, help and healing, so that His love may flow out to them through us and our actions. When we become instruments of God's love, there is no limit to what we can accomplish. In God's divine plan, we can become the sanctuary of the weary and heavy-laden; we can, with our efforts, become a source of sweet, refreshing waters in the wilderness that is this world.

Here is a story associated with the *Mahabharat*: it pertains to the grand *Ashwameda Yagna* performed by Yudhishtira to mark his coronation as the undisputed king of Hastinapur.

When the sacrifice was over and the priests had been amply rewarded for their participation, a few of the rishis who had stayed on in the yagnashala *saw a mongoose enter the hall. It was indeed a strange creature! One half of its body shone as molten gold, while the other half was a drab brown. The creature made its way to the remains of the* yagna *fire and jumped into the fire-pit, rolling around in the ashes and embers. It emerged from the pit, examined itself, and then went away, looking very disappointed.*

Unable to contain their surprise, the rishis *stopped the mongoose and asked him, "What brings you here to Raja Yudhishtira's court? How is it that one half of your body shines like gold? Why did you roll yourself in the fire-pit? What did you expect from it?"*

The mongoose replied, "Sometime ago, I happened to witness another sacrifice, at which one half of my body turned to gold. Ever since then, I have been looking to attend another ritual, equally worthy, that the other half of my form may also turn golden. When I heard about Raja Yudhishtira's Ashwameda Yagna, *I thought that this might just be what I was looking for. But as you can see, it didn't work like the other one."*

By now the rishis *were thoroughly intrigued. What could be the ritual or sacrifice that was more powerful than the just concluded* yagna *at Hastinapur? Overcome by curiosity, they asked the mongoose to tell them about this ritual.*

"It happened three months ago, in the humble cottage of a poor brahmin," said the mongoose. "The family had hardly anything to eat. But an alms-seeker arrived at the door, and

the brahmin gave all the food away, while his family starved without complaining. After the guest had eaten, I happened to roll on the leaves that were thrown out, and found that the part of my body which touched the leaves, turned into gold. Ever since then, I have been looking to attend a sacrifice of equal magnitude that may help to make my body fully golden."

The stunned rishis *realised that it was not the magnitude and pomp of a sacrifice that made it special!*

LOVE THY
NEIGHBOUR

Rabbi Hillel was a notable 1st Century Jewish teacher. Someone asked the rabbi to teach him everything about the *Torah* while standing on one foot. Rabbi Hillel responded: "What is hateful to you, don't do unto your neighbour. The rest is commentary. Now, go and study."

There is a simple question that all saints ask of us: How can we claim that we love God, if we do not love our fellow human beings? How can we call ourselves human beings if we just watch our brothers and sisters suffering and struggling?

This is what Sri Ramakrishna and Swami Vivekananda emphasised in their teachings: that in this troubled world of pain and suffering, the traditional approach to personal liberation through prayer and meditation is not enough to realise God; one must also take the vow of service to others to experience God fully. Swami Vivekananda tells us that, service to the living God in man (and woman) is the goal of life.

God is Absolute Love—and if we love God, we must be imbued with the longing to serve our fellow men. I believe that true service is a spiritual activity, which at its best, is born out of the love of God. It was a true saint of God who said: Prayer without work is as bad as work without prayer!

God cannot be satisfied with our adoration and devotion if they come only from our lips—for words and alphabets cannot make a prayer. It is our hearts and our own lives that must bear witness to our devotion—and what better way to achieve this than through the service of our fellow beings?

It is possible that some of you may be really overcome by doubts and anxiety when I talk about service to humanity; you may think to yourself, "After all, we are not millionaires. We are people with limited means at our disposal. How can we aspire to serve suffering humanity?"

God can use the least of us in great acts of service, when He so wills. When Jesus fed the five thousand people who had followed him into the hills, he did not use his chief disciples, the apostles as they were called later. In fact, they were full of tension and anxiety, and planning to send the crowds away. Instead, Jesus turned to a small boy whose mother had packed a simple lunch for him. But this boy was willing to give all he had in perfect trust to the Master. I am sure there were many wealthy people in the crowd who had better food with them, but I doubt if they had the faith, trust and devotion of the little boy, who was willing to give his lunch away when Jesus asked him to.

This is the great gift of service—it blesses him who receives and him who serves!

"What do we live for if not to make the world less difficult for each other?" asks the distinguished writer and novelist, George Eliot. Most of us are inclined to be self-centered, and to live narrow, selfish lives—but it is only in selfless living that we can discover the best that we are capable of. And do not restrict 'giving' to the giving of alms, giving money to the poor! You were surely made for higher things—so give of yourself, give of your time, talents and energies to lighten the loads of the weary and the heavy-laden!

Albert Schweitzer was always pained to hear people say, "If only I were rich, I would do great things to help and serve others." He would point out to them that all of us could be rich in love and generosity, and that we could always give our loving interest and concern to others—which is worth more than all the money in the world!

THE VALUE OF LOVE AND COMPASSION

Nowadays, we use the word 'philanthropist' to describe a multi-millionaire who donates vast sums of money to charitable organisations. Many of us do not know that *'philanthropist'* is derived from two Greek words, *'philas'*, which means loving, and *'anthropos'*, which is man. In other words, the root meaning of philanthropist is a loving man. Aren't we all capable of becoming philanthropists? Of course we are—if we give of ourselves, from a heart filled with love.

"If you want others to be happy, practise compassion," the Dalai Lama tells us.

In loving and compassionate service, in selfless and caring service lies the secret of a peaceful, united world community.

A woman once wrote to evangelist Billy Graham, saying that her life had become empty after her children had grown up and left home. She was filled with gloom—she felt lonely and useless.

Billy Graham pointed out to her that until then, her immediate family had utilised all her time and energy. Now, it was time for her to further extend the range and scope of her love. He reminded her of children who needed understanding and care in her community; he spoke of old people who needed companionship. "Why don't you get out of your narrow circle and find the joy of helping others?" he asked her.

A few days later, she wrote back to him, "I tried your prescription. It worked! I have walked from night into day!"

Of course charity begins at home, but it need not stay put there! Extend your service to society, the community in which you live. Let your community reach out to others—and you will find that the whole world is soon linked by the spirit of selfless service!

Once, a devotee approached Shirdi Sai Baba and said to him, "Baba, give me the gift of Brahma Gyan. *For I know, that it is you alone who can give it to me."*

Sai Baba nodded his head and turned to another disciple and asked him to buy some food from the bazaar *for a hungry beggar who was crying for alms. This disciple did not have any money. Baba asked the devotee, "Can you lend me some money to buy food for this hungry brother?"*

The devotee was abashed and said he had very little money with him. "Never mind," said Baba. "Bring what little you can and offer it to the poor man."

The following day, this devotee returned with the same plea, "Baba, give me the gift of Brahma Gyan. *For I know, that it is you alone who can give it to me."*

This time, Baba looked him in the eye and said to him,

"Yesterday, you heard me asking you for money to get food for a hungry one. You had fifty rupees in your pocket, but deliberately said you had very little money. How can you ask to attain to Brahma Gyan, *the highest Truth, when you don't care about the immediate need of your fellow human being?"*

Mother Teresa would often say to her helpers,"Let everyone who comes to you return to their life feeling better and happier." If we all tried to follow this simple precept, wouldn't this world be a better and happier place?

We all have something to give! Let us give with love and compassion, and we will make the world a better place!

THE LIFE
BEAUTIFUL

Gurudev Sadhu Vaswani once narrated the story of a seeker, who wanted to learn the secret of the Life Beautiful. It was taught to him by an old man, whose face was radiant with the light of joy and peace. The old man said to the seeker, "From morn till night I seek to serve. I am busy, busy, working for others, trying to help others, trying to serve the poor, sending out my sympathy and love to those who stand in need of help and strength, serving them in this broken world."

The young seeker was thrilled. Suddenly, this discovery shone within his heart – that the others were not apart from him, but only parts of a Great Whole. "They are mine, as I am theirs," he said to himself. "No separation between me and the poor and suffering ones, between me and the lowly ones! We are one! We are brothers!"

Thus did he discover the secret of the Life Beautiful which was nothing but sympathy and compassion that went out to all.

How can I refrain from quoting those beautiful lines that have never failed to inspire me!

I shall pass through this life but once.
Any good, therefore, that I can do
Or any kindness that I can show to any fellow creature,
Let me do it now.
Let me not defer or neglect it,
For I shall not pass this way again.

Don't hold back! Don't underestimate yourself and your abilities! Don't imagine that you cannot make a difference! We may feel that our effort is but a drop in the ocean—yet every drop counts in the ocean of service!

"The world, I believe is a garden of God. God is in all that is — men and women, birds and animals, fish and fowl, worms and insects, in trees and flowers, in rivers and rocks, in stones and stars.**"**

- J.P.V.

MAN
AND HIS
HABITAT

The philosophical foundation of compassion in Hinduism is rooted in the Vedantic ideal of the One Life in All Creation. "All that is, is a vesture of the Lord", proclaims the *Isa Upanishad.* The concept of the Brahman, or Universal Soul, encompasses the entirety of existence. Since all aspects of existence are part of this Universal Soul, Hindus believe that the Divine is manifested in every living being. This leads to the ideal of Reverence for all life, and its corollary, *daya* or compassion, and *ahimsa* or non-violence.

Gurudev Sadhu Vaswani often spoke of *prakriti sanga*—fellowship with nature—as essential to human happiness. I recall his teaching: "God dwells in all nature—therefore let us cultivate reverence for nature! Reverence for our rivers and forests; reverence for our lakes and waterfalls; reverence for trees and plants and the grass that grows beneath our feet; reverence for birds and animals, whom I love to call our younger brothers and sisters in the One family of Creation."

I love to point out to my friends that Sri Krishna's love was not restricted to the *Gopas* and *Gopis* of Brindavan. He loved the very grass and trees and the stones and the by-lanes of Brindavan. That is why, to this day, pious devotees still walk barefoot when they go for their Brindavan *darshan!* Krishna's love was for every creature, every tree, every plant, and every stone. And so we see Krishna is always depicted, sitting on a stone, under a tree, by the side of a cow. It shows Krishna's love for all of nature. Krishna is shown as playing the flute on the banks of the river Yamuna. The river is symbolic of the pure spirit of the universe, the ever-flowing energy of the universe!

When Ved Vyasa's wife conceived their son, Shuka, and he was a foetus in the mother's womb, he decided not to be born upon this earth, which was infested with maya. *It is said that he stayed unborn for sixteen long years, not wanting to be misled by the material illusions of this world. But Rishi Vyasa wanted a son desperately, and so the Lord suspended* maya *temporarily, so that Shuka could take birth. He was born a handsome, intelligent, fully grown youth of sixteen. Such was the birth of this great* gnani, *who was a brilliant* yogi *with astounding powers and deep knowledge. And the moment he was born, he decided to set out in search of a* tapobana, *not wishing to be entrapped by familial bonds.*

Sage Vyasa ran after the young man, calling out, "Shuka, stop! My beloved son, come back to me!"

Shuka did not stop or look back even once. But it is said that the trees and animals, the very rocks and stones and creepers all around them, spoke to Vyasa, "Father, do not try to stop me, for I go in search of the Truth that will liberate me!" Such was Shuka's sense of identification with the Divinity in all creation. In Sanskrit, this is called ekatmabhava – *or the ability to behold the One in all.*

This is a precious personal memory that I am sharing with you. In my younger days, I loved to accompany Gurudev Sadhu Vaswani on his evening walks. On one such walk, I saw a large, sharp-edged stone obstructing his path. Eager to be of service to the Master, I hastily stepped forward and kicked the stone aside, lest it should hurt his feet.

The moment I turned back, I knew I had done something wrong. For, there was a look of pain in Gurudev Sadhu Vaswani's eyes.

"What is it, Dada?" I asked him humbly. "Have I said or done something which I should not have done? If so, pray forgive me!"

In answer to my question, Gurudev Sadhu Vaswani posed another question, which is etched in my mind and heart to this day. With characteristic insight, he said to me: "If God dwells in the scripture, who dwells in the stone?"

I imbibed the great value of Reverence for all things, animate and inanimate, from the Master that day. I resolved then, that I would treat everything, everyone, with respect, love and reverence.

MOTHER
NATURE

Reverence for Mother Earth and all of creation is part of the *dharma,* the code of conduct or way of life enjoined by our ancient scriptures. The *Bhumi Sukta* (Earth Hymn) in the *Atharva Veda* is amazing in the ecological and environmental values it places before us. Let me quote to you the opening verses of this beautiful hymn which emphasises that the Earth is supported not just by gravitational force, but by the power of Truth, *Dharma* and *Tapasya*:

Truth, Eternal Order that is great and stern, Consecration, Austerity, Prayer and Ritual – these uphold the Earth. May she, Queen of what has been and will be, make a wide world for us. (1)

Earth which has many heights, and slopes and the unconfined plains that bind men together, Earth that bears plants of various healing powers, may she spread wide for us and thrive. (2)

Earth, in which lie the sea, the river and other waters, in which food and cornfields have come to be, in which live all that breathes and that moves, may she confer on us the finest of her yield. (3)

Mistress of four quarters, in whom food and cornfields have come to be, who bears in many form the breathing and moving life, may she give us cattle and crops. (4)

Earth, in which men of old before us
performed their various work,
where devas *overwhelmed the* asuras,
Earth, the home of kine, horses, birds,
may she give us magnificence and lustre.(5)

All life is one! This has been the one great truth instilled into me by my Master, Gurudev Sadhu Vaswani. The life that sleeps in stones and minerals, the life that stirs in plants and trees, the life that dreams in animals and birds, is the same life that wakes and breathes in man. Every spark of life is of the universal spirit.

Let me quote to you the beautiful opening *sloka* of the *Shanti Sukta* from the *Atharva Veda*:

Om Shanta dhyou
Shanta prithvi
Shantam idam uranthariksham
Shanta udhanvatirapa
Shantana sant aushadi

May peace prevail in the skies
May peace prevail on earth
May peace prevail in vast space
May peace prevail in the flowing river, and in plants and trees!

Are we at one with the invocation of the *rishis*? Are we, today, at peace with nature? Are we giving our global village, our habitat the reverence it deserves? I request each one of you to answer it in your own personal capacity!

I am aware that the fashionable, trendy words to use today are 'ecology' or 'environment'. But I chose the word nature, deliberately, because it is close to my heart. It is a term that is known and loved by millions of men and women worldwide. It is associated with peace, purity, serenity, unspoiled beauty, tranquility and the transcendental spirit of the universe. It recalls to my mind the *pancha tattwa*, the five elements—earth, water, fire, air and space—of which our universe is composed. It encompasses these myriad aspects of creation, hundreds of thousands of living beings and organisms, those stunningly beautiful landscapes, mountains, rivers, seas, forests, deserts, mangroves, lakes and plains that man could not have made—but alas, which he seems to be destroying irrationally!

In my old fashioned way, I have always loved to call her "Mother Nature". But I doubt if we have the right to call ourselves her children anymore! We are actually a vital component of nature, and it is our sacred obligation to preserve and protect this planet that God has given to us as a habitat. Alas, we live upon earth as if there is no tomorrow—as if we care nothing for unborn generations who will continue to live here long after we are gone!

As the crown of God's creation, we should have been guardians, protectors, wardens of nature. Instead, we have exploited her shamelessly, selfishly—and O, so foolishly. We must learn to live at peace with nature, we must cultivate a symbolic relationship with her—or we will hurtle down the abyss of self-destruction.

And how can we condone or justify the way we treat animals—our younger brothers and sisters in the one family of creation, whom we are morally obliged to protect! O, the sin of daily slaughter in our cities! How can we have peace on earth until we stop all killing?

Among all the creatures on earth, man alone has the capacity to interfere with the ecological balance. Elephants do not – cannot – destroy forests and uproot trees; tigers and lions do not destroy their own habitats; birds and insects do not pollute the air, any more than fishes pollute rivers and seas.

It is man's responsibility to protect the environment, preserve the ecological balance. It is his sacred duty to see that the integrity and diversity of nature is maintained. For, to destroy nature, is to destroy mankind.

If civilisation is to endure,
it must be built in a new spirit of reverence,
in a new religion of reverence for all life. **"**

- J.P.V.

REVERENCE
FOR ALL
LIFE

Reverence for nature is essential. Reverence for nature will help us to survive upon this planet. Reverence for nature will help us to preserve and protect this blessed earth for our children—and our children's children.

Reverence is essential—reverence for our rivers and forests; reverence for our lakes and waterfalls; reverence for trees and plants and the grass that grows beneath our feet; reverence for birds and beasts, whom I love to call our younger brothers and sisters.

My vision of unity and fellowship and brotherhood is of a world in which the right to life is accorded to every creature that breathes the breath of life! How can wars cease until we stop all killing? How can we claim to seek world peace when we continue to slaughter sentient creatures?

Have you ever spared a thought for the atrocities that are perpetrated on the animals day after day, in laboratories and in slaughterhouses? Have you thought of these creatures imprisoned in their tiny cages, deprived of light, fresh air and free movement, compelled to stand and live in their own filth? Have you thought of animals 'stunned' and then hung upside down in a line to have their throats slit? And after this appalling treatment, they are finally eaten up—consumed! And this nightmare goes on, day after day.

My friends, let me tell you, we cannot speak of *dharma*, we cannot speak of creation as one family until we stop the exploitation of animals—until we stop all killing! All killing must be stopped for the simple reason that if man kills an animal for food, he will not hesitate to kill a fellow human being whom he regards as an enemy.

We cannot have a world family built on the exploitation of the poor, and on the blood of the dumb, defenseless creatures! Such a 'family' will only crumble beneath the burden of its own weight. The new global village, the new family of humanity must be built on a nobler, worthier ideal. If civilisation is to endure, it must be built in a new spirit of reverence, in a new religion of reverence for all life.

Animal welfare is not enough! We must speak of animal rights! Men have their rights; have animals no rights? I believe the time has come when all animal lovers must get together and formulate a charter of animal rights—a charter of man's duty towards the animal kingdom. I hope and pray that India—the country of the Buddha, Mahavira, Mahatma Gandhi and Sadhu Vaswani—will be first among nations to pass an enactment giving rights to animals.

Every animal has its fundamental rights. And the very first right of every animal is the right to live! We cannot take away that which we cannot give! And since we cannot give life to a dead creature, we have no right to take away the life of a living one!

The time is come when we must decide once and for all that all types of exploitation must cease. We must recognise the moral inviolability of individual rights—both human and non-human. Just as black people do not exist as resources for white people, just as the poor do not exist as resources for rich, just as women don't exist as resources for men, even so animals don't exist as resources for human beings! In the words of my Revered Master, Sadhu Vaswani, "No nation can be free, until its animals are free!"

We cannot call this world our own family until all forms of exploitation cease!

SERVICE
BEFORE
SELF!

The cement that binds a family together and keeps the bonds always glued together is the spirit of selfless love and service. What is applicable to our blood ties must also apply to the world family!

Ralph Waldo Emerson urges us to realise that we can leave the world a better place in many simple ways—by producing a healthy child, by creating a clean, green patch of garden, or by a reformed social condition. Even if one person breathes easier because of you, it makes a difference! There is always some work that will never be done if you don't do it; someone who would miss you if you were gone; somewhere there is a place which you alone can fill!

You can make a difference. Let me give you the words of Bertrand Russell: "It may seem to you conceited to suppose that you can do anything important towards improving the lot of mankind. But this is a fallacy. You must believe that you can help bring about a better world. A good society is produced only by good individuals, just as truly as a majority in a presidential election is produced by the votes of single electors."

We regard ourselves as responsible citizens. We pay our taxes and our bills on time; we exercise our franchise and fulfill our democratic duties; we try to obey all traffic rules; we steer clear of breaking the laws of the land; we try not to interfere in other people's affairs . . .

But this is not enough! Doing our duty is alright – but we need to do our duty and a little more! The opposite of love is not hate but indifference, or apathy—to the needs of those around us. We need to contribute our share—our mite—to the welfare of the world; to what Sri Krishna calls *lokasangraha*.

Little drops of water make the mighty ocean! Little grains of sand make this beautiful land. So too, when we all perform little acts of service, little deeds of kindness, the world will become a better place.

Let us turn for inspiration to St. Francis's prayer:

Lord, make me an instrument of thy Peace,
Where there is hatred let me sow love
Where there is injury, pardon;
Where there is discord, let me bring truth,
Where there is doubt, faith;
Where there is despair, let me bring hope
Where there are shadows, may I bring thy Light;
Where there is sadness, let me bring joy.
Lord, grant that I may seek rather to comfort than be comforted;
To understand, than be understood;
To love, than be loved;
For it is by giving that one receives,
It is by forgetting self, that one finds,
It is by forgiving, that one is forgiven
It is by dying that one awakens to eternal life.

66 When the darkness of ignorance is dispelled
by the first glimmer of understanding,
we will realize that different races and different
nations are members of one global family. **99**

- J.P.V.

THE
GLOBAL
FAMILY

Every morning in Indian schools, children recite the prayer of unity which begins thus:

India is my country. All Indians are my brothers and sisters.
I love my country and I am proud of its rich and varied heritage.
I shall always strive to be worthy of it.
I shall give my parents, teachers and all elders respect
and treat everyone with courtesy.
To my country and my people, I pledge my devotion.
In their wellbeing and prosperity alone lies my happiness.

Considering the fact that we are now beginning to call our world a 'global village', I think it is also time we modify this prayer thus:

The world is my family, and all human beings are my brothers and sisters.
I love my world and I am proud of its rich and varied heritage.
I shall always strive to be worthy of it.
I shall give my parents, teachers, and all human beings respect and treat everyone with courtesy.
To my world, my country and my fellow human beings, I pledge my devotion.
In their wellbeing and prosperity alone lies my happiness.

Does this not sound beautiful?

I am told that there is a magnificent archaeological site in Western Africa – the vast ruins of Jenne in Mali. Apparently, this was a city of over 100,000 people one thousand years ago. It was, in fact, a world class metropolis in the first millennium, far surpassing London in size and importance.

A visitor to the site observes: "Its art was stunning. Its architecture reflected a complex society . . . What struck me most, however, was the fact that it had been completely ignored by western archeologists for decades, because they found no evidence of military constructions! The Jenne civilisation did not find its strength through military conquest or intimidation of its people, but through co-operation! It was a great city built not on fear, but friendship!"

Mary Baker Eddy, the founder of the distinguished newspaper, *The Christian Science Monitor,* wrote of her vision of the brotherhood of humanity in 1908: "For many years, I have prayed daily that there be no more war, no more barbarous slaughter of our fellow human beings; prayed that all the people of the earth . . . love God supremely, and love their neighbours as themselves."

If mankind was created by God, is not our brotherhood an established fact?

I said to you earlier, this world is a garden of God. God is in all that is—men and women, birds and animals, fish and fowl, worms and insects, in trees and flowers, in rivers and rocks, in stones and stars, in this pen that scribbles, and even the paper on which my moving fingers write, "Krishna! Krishna." Krishna is in all—and we all are in Krishna! When we have this vision of the One-in-all and All-in-one, we will grow in the spirit of Brotherhood of all creation!

Is not this the vision of the One-in-all, given to us in the Vedas? Sri Krishna tells us the same thing in His song Divine, the Bhagavad Gita:

> *Who sees Me*
> *Deathlessly dwelling*
> *In all that is,*
> *And who sees*
> *All in Me —*
> *Of him I shall not lose hold*
> *Nor shall he lose hold of Me!*

Our hearts need to be saturated with love, for love is the light which will illumine the world. For this, developed brains are not needed; we need illumined hearts that can behold the vision of fellowship, unity and brotherhood. Love is what we need to build a new humanity, a new world of brotherhood and peace. We must eliminate the dark forces of greed, selfishness, prejudice and mistrust—and cultivate the power of love which is also the power of peace!

LOVE
IS THE
SOLUTION
TO ALL OUR
PROBLEMS!

All over the world, today, there is a cry for a new world order; a new life. For men and women, young and old are tired of the present order. The cry comes from temples and churches, from factories and farms, from homes and offices, from souls seeking peace, and hearts full of aspirations for a better future.

But let me tell you—there is hope for us all! I believe a new age is dawning, a new age in which love and peace will be established upon this earth. I don't merely believe it, I can almost hear the new age knocking on the doors of our hearts. All we need are the blessed ones who will open the door to the new age!

I am convinced that we are standing on the threshold of a new age of love and peace that will see all nations and all people united by the bonds of brotherhood.

Today, we have arrived at a stage where, nations and individuals alike must learn to understand one another—to love one another, to dwell in peace with one another or perish! There is no other choice!

The very first note on the musical scale of peace is Love. We must love all—not merely our family and friends, our kith and kin—we must love all creation.

We must cultivate the fine art of friendship; we must make

friends with all – for the permanent peace plan can only be a friendship plan. Therefore, we must go out and make friends with people belonging to different religions, different communities and nationalities. This is what friendship is all about; not just sticking to the people you know, your neighbours, your colleagues, the people you grew up with.

Let me ask you a question: When you go out for a walk, do you smile at the people whom you meet on the way? Some people will smile back at you; some people will not return your smile, but you have not lost anything! But you may win new friends with your smile—and that's what the world needs: Bridges of friendship between people, communities and nations.

Each one of us can become an ambassador of peace, a harbinger of peace, merely by smiling the smile of friendship. We can become smile millionaires if we keep on smiling, smiling, smiling.

Sometimes, when I am addressing audiences in different cities, I am struck by the fact that everybody appears to be so serious, so earnest, that they forget to smile! Some of them are even busy taking down notes of the points I make—but they seem unaware of their neighbours, the people seated right next to them.

I stop then and there, and request everyone: "Please turn to either side and smile at those who are sitting beside you." You have to see the visible difference it makes in the auditorium! Suddenly, a crowd of solemn strangers turns into a happy group of friends! The relaxation, the release of tension is so palpable! I have heard it said that a meeting was so tense that you could cut the tension with a knife. Well, when people smile at each other, the waves of friendship that arise can almost be felt, lapping gently around you, easing out all the tension!

Alas, we seem to have forgotten how to smile! Someone said to me the other day that constant frowning actually causes wrinkles on the face, but even that doesn't stop some people from frowning!

On the bus, in the train, in the elevator, in the supermarket, at the lunch counter—smile at the people standing before you, behind you and next to you. You will have made at least four friends and paved the way to peace! So it is that George Eliot tells us: "What sunshine is to flowers, smiles are to humanity. They are but trifles, but when scattered along life's pathway, the good they do is inconceivable!"

A generous dose of humour always goes a long way to make life feel good! Once, a pompous and arrogant professor was walking along a very narrow street when he came face to face with a rival professor. The street was too narrow for two to pass. The professor pulling himself up to his full height, said haughtily: "I never make way for fools!" Smiling, the rival stepped aside and said: "I always do."

I often say to myself that the day on which I have not made a new friend is a lost day indeed! When all the people of the world become friends with each other, there will be no wars!

"Friendship with all?" one of you might object. "Isn't that a bit impractical? A friend is someone who has proved himself to you—tried and tested in the trials of life. How can we cultivate friendship with anyone and everyone?" This is just the trouble with us: all our ideals and values, all our great truths and teachings, we prefer to keep as theories and paper prescriptions. We imagine that they are for intellectual consumption and not to be put into practice. This gap between precept and practice must be closed with immediate effect!

I repeat: we must learn to *love* each other; *love* as in the Commandment: Thou shalt *love* thy neighbour as thyself. It is this spirit of love that is expressed in the universal bond of the global family. If we pick and choose and reject, universal brotherhood does not have a chance! As Mother Teresa puts it, "If you judge people, you have no time to love them."

Make no mistake about this: To an Indian, "Love thy neighbour" means loving the people of Pakistan; to an Israeli, "Love thy neighbour" means loving the Palestinians; to Christians, it means loving the Muslims and Hindus and Sikhs!

Let me remind you therefore, of the words of the apostles:

"Bless them that curse you, and pray for your enemies. Fast on behalf of those that prosecute you; for what thanks is there if you love them that love you? ... Do ye love them that hate you, and ye will not have an enemy!"

Can we, as human beings do this?

If we could, we are asserting the Divinity in us—and we are helping to spread God's peace in the world!

Love blesses the one who offers it and the one who receives it. Love can keep you healthy and happy, and help you face the problems of daily life in the right spirit!

FACE
THE
WORLD WITH
LOVE!

There is a superstition held by many of us that a broken or damaged idol or image of worship must be removed and thrown away or dropped in the water to destroy the bad consequences of its break or damage. A man was once about to throw such a damaged idol, a statue of Sri Krishna into a river, when a friend stopped him. "If your father, mother or son were to break a limb or suffer a fracture, would you throw them out of the house?" he asked the man.

"But this is different," stammered the man. "This is only an idol... and it is damaged."

"Is not Sri Krishna a member of your family? Don't you offer Him *naivedya*, before you eat? Don't you take your problems to Him everyday? Don't you pray to Him? Is He not the head of your household? How can you throw Him out because His image is damaged?"

A young soldier was finally coming home after having fought in Vietnam. He called his parents when he landed in San Francisco. "Mom and Dad, I'm coming home, but I've a favour to ask. I have a friend I'd like to bring home with me."

"Sure," they replied, "we'd love to meet him."

"There's something you should know," the son continued, "He was hurt pretty badly in the fighting. He stepped on a

landmine and lost an arm and a leg. He has lost most of his vision and has nowhere else to go. I would like him to come and live with us."

"I'm sorry to hear that, son. Maybe we can help him find somewhere to live."

"No, Mom and Dad, I want him to live with us."

"Son," said the father, "you don't know what you're asking. Someone with such a handicap would be a terrible burden on us. We have our own lives to live, and we can't let something like this interfere with our lives. I think you should just come home and forget about this guy. He'll find a way to live on his own."

At that point, the son hung up the phone. The parents heard nothing more from him. A few days later, however, they received a call from the San Francisco police. Their son had died after falling from a building, they were told. The police believed it was suicide.

The grief-stricken parents flew to San Francisco and were taken to the city morgue to identify the body of their son. They recognised him, but to their horror they also discovered something they didn't know, their son had only one arm and one leg. His eyes were badly injured. He had been referring to his own condition when he spoke of the friend he wanted to bring home!

The parents in this story are like many of us. Their idea of family was confined to their 'comfort level' of their own people, living the way they thought was 'suitable' or 'acceptable'. We find it easy to love those who are good-looking or fun to have around, but we don't like people who inconvenience us or make us feel uncomfortable. We would rather stay away from people who aren't as healthy, beautiful, or smart as we are. Thankfully, God does not treat us that way! He loves us with an unconditional love that welcomes us into the forever family, regardless of how broken, bruised or handicapped we are!

Yes, we must be unafraid to love – for it requires courage. I have always believed that the power of love is far greater than the power of hatred. If we are to confront the dark forces of destruction and annihilation, we must use the greatest weapon in our possession – the power of love.

Love is not weak. Love is not sentimental. And love is not always easy! But let me tell you, the power of love is greater than you think! Most of us, I am afraid are obsessed with the love of Power; we must learn to focus instead on the Power of Love!

THE
POWER
OF
LOVE

The Greeks believe that there are three types of love, three different facets of love manifested in human beings: namely, Eros, Philos and Agape. Let me explain.

Eros is physical, sentimental love that grips two people. It has its good and bad sides, selfish and unselfish aspects. It enables two people, a man and woman to get married and live for each other. However, it may turn to possessiveness, excessive attachment, jealousy and insecurity. In some cases, it may even turn to vicious hatred and hostility, as in the case of a marriage ending in a destructive break-up.

Philos is love as friendship. In the case of elderly couples, philos keeps a happy marriage alive long after the flame of eros has died down. It is love between family and friends. Nevertheless, it is still conditional love; it seeks something for itself from the loved one, family member or friend – be it companionship, loyalty, support or trust.

Agape is unselfish, unconditional love. It is a complete and all-consuming experience in itself. It was the kind of love that Jesus recommended to us when he urged us, "Love thy neighbour as thyself." The Rev. Dr. Martin Luther King Jr. also used the Greek term "agape" to describe a universal love that "discovers the neighbour in every man it meets". It is said that those rare beings who feel agape in its highest form, become ascetics, hermits and renounce the world to seek the ultimate vision of unity which we call *Samadhi*.

They choose the life of isolation and contemplation in which they find the bliss of *Samadhi*. The others who are capable of such love, choose a life of active participation with the human family, a life of loving service filled with enthusiasm and boundless compassion and selflessness.

FACE IT
WITH LOVE!
PRACTICAL
SUGGESTIONS

1

THE
GOLDEN
RULE

Follow the Golden Rule that is the foundation of all religious scriptures and teachings: Do unto others what you would have others do unto you!

Gurudev Sadhu Vaswani said to us, "There is the great Cosmic Law that what you do comes back to you. What you do unto others, you do unto yourselves. Therefore be kind to all, if you will be truly happy."

The great German philanthropist, Oberlin, was one day caught in a blinding snowstorm. He could not see a thing in front of him. He cried out for help but his shrieks were lost in the angry wind. Exhausted, he dropped down unconscious on the snow.

A peasant happened to pass by and, finding a fellow human lying unconscious on the snow, carried him in his arms to the warmth of his hut. There, Oberlin revived. Looking into the eyes of his saviour, he said, "You have saved my life. I want to give you a rich reward."

"A reward? What for?" asked the peasant in surprise. "I saw a fellow human being in distress and brought him to my hut. I have only done my duty."

"At least tell me your name," pleaded Oberlin. The peasant smiled. "Tell me, friend, is the name of the Good Samaritan mentioned anywhere in the Bible?"

Oberlin pondered for a minute, and then answered, "No, it is not."

"Then," said the peasant, "let me withhold mine."

Many of us are under the impression that "acts of service" are grand and noble, and involve doing something spectacular and sensational – like saving someone's life. Not all of us are called upon to perform heroic acts. But it would be wonderful if we were not found wanting, when we are called upon to act. We may not always be able to do exceptional deeds, but there are thousands of small, generous acts we can do, to help others lift the load on the rough road of life.

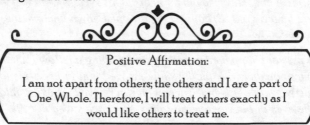

Positive Affirmation:

I am not apart from others; the others and I are a part of One Whole. Therefore, I will treat others exactly as I would like others to treat me.

" In God's divine plan,
we can become the sanctuary
of the weary and heavy-laden;
we can, with our efforts,
become a source of sweet,
refreshing waters in the
wilderness that is this world. **"**

- J.P.V.

2
RISE
IN
LOVE

People often talk of 'falling' in love; you must rise in love. Therefore, establish a firm and loving relationship with God, first and foremost. Make God your father or mother, your friend or brother. Let everything you do strengthen this relationship with God.

Bhakta Prahlada established such a relationship with God at a very young age! Prahlada was born a great Hari-bhakta *and a* Dharmatma. *His mind and heart and soul were filled with devotion to Hari.*

His father Hiranyakashipu was determined to wipe out all traces of Hari-bhakti *from his kingdom. He used his demonic power to commit every form of* adharma; *he tortured sadhus and sages; he harassed the virtuous and the pious. He began to act as if he were God. He even insisted that he should be worshipped by the people of his kingdom. On pain of death, people were forbidden to utter the Name of Hari.*

Prahlada refused to be cowed down by his father's threats and coercion; the Name of Hari was on his lips constantly. Hiranyakashipu was so incensed by his son's Hari-bhakti *that he put the little boy through the most excruciating torture. Prahlada was thrown down from cliffs: he was sent to be trampled underfoot by wild elephants; his father even attempted to have the boy thrown into a fire to burn him alive; and cast away into the ocean to drown to his death.*

But the child was a true devotee of the Lord; and true to his role as deena bandhu, *Sri Hari saved him from all the compounded evil and multiple tortures inflicted by his cruel father. And the name of Hari never ever left his lips or his heart.*

You all know the familiar story from the Puranas: *the Lord came down as Narasimha, to protect the child from his father's wrath and torture. The Narasimha avatara is not just a manifestation of the Lord's rage and destructive power. He is not a Deity to be feared or worshipped at arm's length. His incarnation is also an assurance to His devotees that no matter how trying the circumstances, He will always rush to their aid. Ugra Narasimha is also Prahlada Varada, He who incarnated to protect His devotee from harm. As Lakshmi Narasimha, with the Divine Mother by his side, He is the symbol of protective, fatherly love. We must also remember, that* bhakti *is not a matter of birth or lineage; it is a matter of character and environment. Prahlada became renowned as a* dharmatma, *a king who governed his subjects according to the laws of* dharma. *Born an* asura *(literally, one not in harmony with the universe), he demonstrated that the way of devotion is open to all.*

When you have established such a relationship, you will find it natural to offer the love of your heart to everything and everyone around you. For if we are all God's children, we will surely learn to accept and love each other as we are and in spite of what we are.

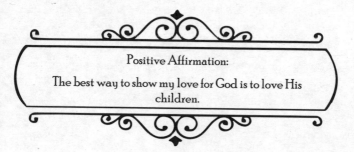

Positive Affirmation:

The best way to show my love for God is to love His children.

3

SPEAK
GENTLY

Speak softly; speak gently; speak with loving kindness. Treat everyone with love and respect. Greet God in everyone you meet. Let others' harsh words and unkindness never drive you to return unkindness for unkindness.

A king once posed a question to the wise men assembled in his darbar: what is the sweetest thing on earth? The king firmly said to his courtiers, "I do not want a text book answer. Your answer should come from your own experience." One of the courtiers seated there answered, "The sweetest thing in this world is honey." The second courtier said, "The sweetest thing is unrefined sugar-candy." The third person answered, "The sweetest thing is sugar." The fourth answer was, "Malai barfi". And many such answers were given.

The king then posed a second question, "Which is the most bitter thing in the world?" "Poison," replied someone. The king immediately chided the person, "Have you ever taken poison? Have you ever experienced its effect? I said, the answers should come from your own experience. A person who has taken poison, cannot be alive."

There were many answers such as karela (bitter gourd), dandelion, mushrooms and so on. At last, one man gave an answer which pleased the king greatly. He said, "Your majesty, the answer to both your questions is one and the same: the sweetest and the most bitter thing on earth is the human tongue. Man can have a sweet tongue or a sharp tongue. A sweet tongue is soothing; it is like a balm. It is the sweetest thing. A sharp tongue hurts and stings. It is the bitterest thing in the world." The king was very pleased with the answer and rewarded the man for the same.

Guru Nanak tells us: Until your speech is sweet, you cannot enter God's domain. The angels at the Gates of Heaven will ask you, "Have you learnt the art of speaking sweetly?" If your answer is yes, then you would be allowed to enter Heaven. If your answer is no, or yes and no – sometimes yes, I speak gently, but sometimes I raise my voice, – then too, you would be stopped. The angels will not allow you in, saying, "First let us calculate your worth in terms of good deeds and then we shall decide on your entry."

There are very many wealthy people who speak harsh words to the people to whom they offer charity. They may give a poor man money and tell him, "Don't show your dirty face to me again!" or they may lose their temper and yell, "Don't be so lazy! Don't expect me to prop you up all the time!" This is not the kind of love or philos that I would recommend! The people we seek to serve are not apart from us – they are a part of us. This sense of identification is very essential for true service. When you serve others, you must identify with them.

Harsh words cause deeper wounds than sticks and stones. The poet-saint, Thiruvalluvar, tells us: burnt flesh and skin heal sooner or later, but the wounds inflicted by a harsh tongue never, ever heal. Why should we be guilty of inflicting such wounds? Therefore, let us resolve to speak gently, softly, sweetly.

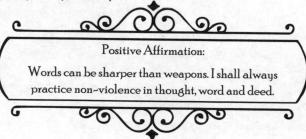

Positive Affirmation:

Words can be sharper than weapons. I shall always practice non-violence in thought, word and deed.

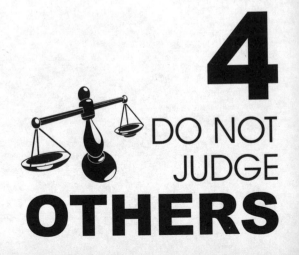

4
DO NOT JUDGE
OTHERS

Stop judging others, for true love is non-judgmental. Do not see the faults of others. When you find fault with others and criticise them harshly, you are drawing negative forces to yourself!

I am told that a tree called the Upas tree grows in certain parts of Indonesia. It grows very thick and it secretes poison so that all forms of vegetation around it are killed. There are people like the Upas tree – they criticise, condemn others; but will not lift a finger to help others improve themselves.

I read about a fashionable, rich young woman, who was taken around a poor locality of New York City. She was disgusted at the sight of the shabbily dressed, unkempt children on the streets. "Look at these dreadful children!" she sneered. "Why can't someone wash and clean them up? Do they have no mothers?"

Her guide explained to her patiently, "Sure, they have mothers who love them – but they don't hate the dirt. You hate the dirt – but you don't love these children. Until the love for the children and hatred for their condition are found together in the same heart, the children will have to remain as they are!"

Positive Affirmation:
I shall always judge others with the same love, compassion and understanding with which I expect God to judge me.

5

LOVE
UNCONDITIONALLY

Learn to love unconditionally. Do not enquire whether he or she deserves your love; for this is trade, bargaining, not love!

I am a great believer in the strength and sustaining power of love: not love that demands, expects, negotiates for something in exchange – but unconditional love that offers itself in understanding, sympathy and compassion. Any other kind of love can only be what the English call 'cupboard love'; which may be a transaction, a bargain, but not the real thing.

An enthusiastic and spirited young lady decided to leave behind her luxurious life in Paris to return to India, the country of her birth, in order to serve the poor villagers and their children in whatever ways she could. On the very first day she drove into a dusty village in her gleaming sports car, filled to the brim with food and toys and chocolates and balloons for the village kids. But the moment she got out of her car and waved to the kids, they all fled from her as if they had seen a witch!

The lady was intelligent. She did not need anyone to tell her the reason for the strange 'reception' she had received. As she stood by her car and gazed into her wing mirror, she realised suddenly what an incongruous figure she must have appeared to be in the eyes of the villagers; branded jeans and T-shirt, bright red lipstick, high heeled sandals and dark goggles that hid most of her face! She had chosen what she thought were comfortable, casual clothes. But she realised that her strange manner of dressing must have intimidated the kids!

Next day, she wore the standard Indian dress of salwar-kurta; *she wore flat sandals and rode an old bicycle to the village temple, where she prayed silently for her mission of love to succeed. She lit a* diya *before the deity, and out of the corner of her eyes, she could see the village children trooping into the temple, staring at her with unabashed curiosity.*

"Didi, aap kaun ho? Aap ka naam kya hai?" (Sister, who are you? What is your name?) asked a little girl. Our young friend smiled and answered in Hindi, that she was new to the village and had come to see if she could make any new friends there. She now opened her bag of toys and gifts, and said, "I came to play with all of you and have some fun."

And now, the children ran to her, crying, "Didi! Can I have a doll?" "Lady, can I have the ball?" "Can you give me some chocolate?" and so on. Her joy knew no bounds. The children had accepted her as one of them!

It is very essential that we have this sense of identification with the people whom we seek to serve.

Positive Affirmation:

My love is unconditional and unqualified by expectations of return.

" Whatever goes out of us,
comes back to us!
Every thought we think,
every word we utter,
every action we perform,
is echoed back into our lives.
Therefore,
send the best out into the world! **"**

- J.P.V.

6
RETURN
LOVE
FOR
HATE

Breathe out love to those who ill-treat you and speak harshly to you! Love your family, love your friends and neighbours; but love those who hate you and criticise you as well! For every blow you receive, give back a blessing. This is not an impossible, impractical precept: it is a sound, wholesome approach to life that will bring lasting peace and happiness to you! For what goes out of you will always come back to you. Send out hostility, mistrust and hatred, and they will come back to you with a vengeance; send out love and peace and friendship; sure enough the Universe will send them back to you like an echo!

There was a little boy who first heard an echo, when he was taken to visit a hill station. He ran up to a scenic valley view point and shouted, "Ho, ho!" and the echo called back, "Ho, ho!" Taken aback, he cried, "Who are you?" and back came the echo, "Who are you?" Startled, the little boy cried out, "I hate you!" and back came the reply, "I hate you!"

The boy ran sobbing to his mother and said, "I don't like this place! There's a bad boy hiding in the hills and he doesn't like me!"

The mother took him back to the ravine and called out, "I love you!" Sure enough the ravine echoed, "I love you!" The boy was amazed. "I love you!" he called out vigorously, wiping away his tears; and then, "Let's become friends!"

This is also the Law of *Karma*; what goes out of you must surely come back to you!

Positive Affirmation:

The love and goodwill that I offer to the world is my greatest treasure.

" If we do anything for the love of God –
it turns out to be the best. Therefore,
every action should be done
in a spirit of offering to the Lord! **"**

- J.P.V.

7

DO IT
FOR
GOD

Whatever you do, whatever you say, whatever you think, whatever you give – do it for the pure love of God! When you live life as an act of love and devotion to God, you will find that you can never do anything which will displease God! Your life will become the life beautiful, the life of love and purity.

There are a hundred and one ways of doing the same thing. Are you a professor teaching in a classroom? Are you a lawyer arguing a case in a court of law? Are you a doctor attending to patients? There are many ways of doing the same thing. Some are right, some are wrong. But only one is the best! And because you are doing everything for the love of God, because you are doing everything as an offering unto the Lord, you must do your work in the best way possible.

Of a holy man, it is said, that he was pained to see suffering and misery, wherever he turned. In deep despair, he cried out to God: "O Lord! They call you the God of Love and Mercy. How can you bear to see so much suffering and yet do nothing about it?"

From the depth of his consciousness, he heard God's voice tell him: "I did do something. I created you!"

God has created us and poured love into our hearts so that we may alleviate the pain and suffering we see around us.

Let us not curse the darkness. Let us kindle the light of love in our hearts!

God loves you; He wants nothing but the best for you. If you ever doubt it, you have not yet realised the meaning of true love.

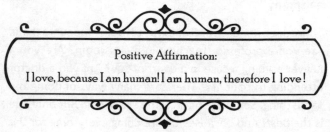

Positive Affirmation:

I love, because I am human! I am human, therefore I love!

66 Keep on forgiving until it hurts!
At least forgive as many times as
you would expect to be forgiven by God. **99**

- J.P.V.

8

FORGIVE
BEFORE
FORGIVENESS IS
ASKED

Learn to forgive others who have harmed you or hurt you in any way. Forgive even before forgiveness is asked. The 'F' of forgiveness is Freedom — freedom from negative emotions, grudges, resentments and bitterness. When these 'blockages' are cleared from your emotional arteries, love flows through your life effortlessly and freely!

Forgiveness brings peace and joy into our life. Forgiveness puts an end to the inner struggle that rages in the soul within, and teaches us to face life with tolerance, understanding and equanimity.

The horrendous Kurukshetra war had just ended. The Kauravas were virtually wiped out. The victorious Pandavas were closeted with Sri Krishna, discussing the implications of their momentous, yet in some ways, tragic victory.

Sri Krishna told the Pandavas and their sons, who occupied two separate tents, to exchange places for the night.

It was a far-sighted, prophetic suggestion. For later that night, Ashwattama, Duryodana's friend and the son of Dronacharya, stole into the Pandava camp on a deadly mission to avenge the death of his slain father and friend. He swooped into what he thought was the tent of the Pandavas, and massacred all Draupadi's sons.

When the distraught mother learnt of the heinous crime, her anguish and anger were beyond control.

Arjuna sought out Ashwattama, vanquished him in single combat and dragged the defeated warrior before his disconsolate wife.

For a moment, murderous hatred flashed in Draupadi's tear-filled eyes – but only for a moment.

She sobered down. It seemed as if she had no more tears to shed. Slowly, she said to Arjuna, "Do not kill him Aryaputra. Let him be spared…let not another mother suffer the bereavement of her child!"

A grievously wronged mother, Draupadi nevertheless empathised with all mothers; this is why she was able to put an end to the struggle that raged within her soul between revenge and forgiveness!

Positive Affirmation:

I shall forgive others' trespasses against me, even as God forgives mine against Him.

"Every individual has his destiny to live through.
Do not imprison anyone:
Do not cling to anyone.
Set everyone free!
That is the meaning of true love!**"**

— J.P.V.

9
LOVE DOES NOT SEEK TO POSSESS

True love is not attachment or possessiveness. Attachment of any kind, as the *Gita* tells us, leads to suffering. *Raga* or *abhinivesha* (clinging and attachment) as it is called, is an impediment – not only on the path of liberation, but also in the attainment of personal happiness. On the other hand, detachment is one of life's greatest lessons for those who seek the true joy of life. In the words of the inspired poet, "If you love someone very dearly, give him wings: let him fly!"

Have you heard of the King who loved his nightingale so dearly that he let it fly to its freedom? He kept the bird in a golden cage in the royal apartment, and would have the bird sing for him everyday. The song was always captivating; but it was so sad, that the king would cry his heart out.

One day, he said to the bird, "Little bird, I am weighed down by the cares and troubles of the kingdom. Can't you, just for once, sing me a happy song, a song of joy and laughter?"

"I could indeed," sighed the bird. "I could sing you a song of the green woods, the wide open spaces and the cloudless, blue sky. But I cannot, cannot sing it from this cage! For that, you must set me free, and allow me to taste the joy of liberation. Then indeed, will I come back to sing to you the happiest song you have ever heard."

"Set you free?" said the king. "I am sure you will take yourself off, and never, ever come back to me."

"If you give me my freedom, how can I treat you in such an ungrateful way? I promise you, I shall come back to you every night, and sing you to sleep with the sweetest and most joyous lullaby you could ever hear."

"Alright," said the king. "I love you far too much to deny you freedom. I shall set you free right away. I do have misgivings that I may never see you again. But I will be happy to know that somewhere, some place, you will be free and singing a happy song."

With a heavy heart, the king opened the door of the cage, stroked the little bird lovingly, carried it to the window, and allowed it to flutter away into the deep woods behind the palace.

There was a great surprise in store for him the next evening. As he returned to his room after a long and tiring day at the court and sank into bed, exhausted, he heard a beautiful song! It came from the window, and he ran to the window to discover his beloved nightingale singing its heart out for him!

"Dear, dear creature," he cried happily, "You came back, you came back to me as you promised!"

"Not just today, but everyday I shall come back to sing for you, O, king," said the grateful bird. "You gave me the greatest of all gifts, the gift of freedom. How can I not keep up my promise to you!"

And so it came to pass that the little nightingale came to sing for the king every night, filling his heart and his life with sheer joy!

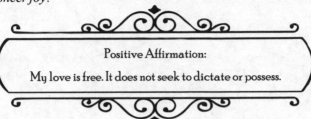

Positive Affirmation:

My love is free. It does not seek to dictate or possess.

10

LOVE IS SELFLESS

The law of love is the law of selfless service and compassion. Therefore, go out of your way to help others. And rejoice in everything that the Will of God brings to you.

Sadhu Hiranand was an ideal teacher. It was in his academy that my beloved Gurudev, Sadhu Vaswani was admitted as a student. He instilled in the mind of his pupils, the ideals of unity and brotherhood, selfless service and compassion for all. He would often tell his students, "You who belong to different classes, different castes and communities, you are all children of the one Father, God!"

He was the founder and head of a popular school; but he also learnt homeopathy and became a qualified doctor, so that he could serve the poor.

Once, a terrible cholera epidemic broke out in Hyderabad-Sind; it spread throughout the city, causing widespread suffering and death. Sadhu Hiranand moved, like an angel of mercy, from house to house, administering his sweet pills and offering relief to the sick and afflicted. He charged no fees either for his visits or his medicines. And he took no precautions for his own health. God gave him the gift of healing and he used it freely for the benefit of suffering humanity. It was said in those days, that 99% of patients who took pills from him, were saved from the jaws of death.

One night, he returned home, famished and tired after his rounds. He felt hungry and asked for food. As he was about to take the first morsel, a knock was heard on the door.

"Who is there?" called out Hiranand.

"We need you urgently," called out a stranger, "we have a cholera stricken brother who is dying."

Sadhu Hiranand returned the morsel held in his hand to the plate, got up, took his medicine chest and without a minute's delay, set out to attend to the patient.

His elder brother, Sadhu Navalrai, said to him, "Brother, you are weary and hungry. Why can't you ask the man to wait and take some food before you leave?"

"It may be too late, if I took a few minutes to eat," replied Hiranand, and he was gone.

Love is the key! Love is the *mantra* that can make the concept of the world family a reality.

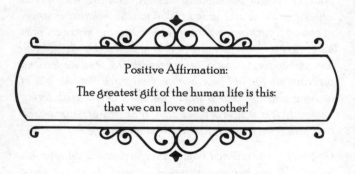

Positive Affirmation:

The greatest gift of the human life is this:
that we can love one another!